鼠 牛 虎 兔 龍 蛇

Chinese Love Signs

馬 羊 猴 鷄 犬 豬

by
Emily Lee

Cover Design – Dennis Garrity
Interior – Janice L. Marchant

JOHN - JAN - 14 - 1947 - DOG - YANG
KATHY - OCT. - 7 - 1951 - RABBIT - YIN
BRENDA - NOV 2 - 1970 - DOG - YANG
CHRISTY - NOV. 1 - 1978 - HORSE - YANG
MIKE - APRIL - 20 - 1982 - DOG - YANG
BRYAN - July - 12, 1984 - RAT - YANG
MATT Sept. 17, 1985 - OX - YIN

CONTENTS

Introduction 7
How to Find Your Sign............9
A Brief Look At the Signs 13
The Rat 20
The Ox 26
The Tiger................................32
The Rabbit..............................38
The Dragon 44
The Snake 50
The Horse................................56
The Goat 62
The Monkey............................68
The Rooster.............................74
The Dog 80
The Pig 87
Western Counterparts 93
Mismatched Signs 94

INTRODUCTION

***Y**ou* are a Goat, your boyfriend is a Snake, your sister is a Dragon... Hey, wait a minute, you say. Before you get bent out of shape, none of this is a bad thing – not according to Oriental astrology.

The parade of Chinese Love Signs has been used for thousands of years by millions of people. However, it is only within the past 30 years that Westerners have begun to appreciate the wonders of Eastern wisdom.

In Oriental astrology, there are also 12 signs. Instead of being named for heavenly constellations, however, they are named for animals. Thus, although you have a Sun sign in Western astrology, you also have an animal sign in the Chinese, or Oriental, Zodiac.

Oriental signs focus on the year of your birth, as well as the day and the month. So instead of taking 12 *months* to complete its cycle – like our Western Zodiac signs – the Eastern cycle of the Animals takes 12 *years*.

Use the chart on pages 9-12 to determine your Chinese Love Sign, which is based on your birth date. Note that the Oriental calendar does *not* start on January 1.

Chinese Love Signs are an excellent way to see if you are matched to your true love. After you've discovered which animal signs fit you and your mate, check to see what the Oriental Zodiac says about your chances for a long and satisfying romance. They are listed under the headings of "Great," "Just Average" and "Challenging."

You will be able to see quickly and easily how your interests and differences – based on the characteristics of each animal sign – will affect your relationship.

In Oriental astrology, the principles of Yin and Yang also apply. These are indicated after the Animal sign on the birth chart in the next section.

In a nutshell, Yin is feminine and passive. It is associated with water, night and the moon. Yang is masculine – positive, active, associated with day, fire and the sun.

Consider the Yin-Yang of both you and a prospective partner. It's another important ingredient in any recipe for romance.

HOW TO FIND YOUR SIGN

Since the Oriental calendar is based on the movement of the Moon, the year does not always start on January 1, as it does in Western culture. Therefore, we have given the exact dates for each sign, as well as the Yin and Yang aspect.

Feb. 18, 1912 - Feb. 5, 1913:	RAT	YANG
Feb. 6, 1913 - Jan. 25, 1914:	OX	YIN
Jan. 26, 1914 - Feb. 13, 1915:	TIGER	YANG
Feb. 14, 1915 - Feb. 2, 1916:	RABBIT	YIN
Feb. 3, 1916 - Jan. 22, 1917:	DRAGON	YANG
Jan. 23, 1917 - Feb. 10, 1918:	SNAKE	YIN
Feb. 11, 1918 - Jan. 31, 1919:	HORSE	YANG
Feb. 1, 1919 - Feb. 19, 1920:	GOAT	YIN
Feb. 20, 1920 - Feb. 7, 1921:	MONKEY	YANG
Feb. 8, 1921 - Jan. 27, 1922:	ROOSTER	YIN
Jan. 28, 1922 - Feb. 15, 1923:	DOG	YANG
Feb. 16, 1923 - Feb. 4, 1924:	PIG	YIN

Feb. 5, 1924 - Jan. 24, 1925:   RAT   YANG
Jan. 25, 1925 - Feb. 12, 1926: OX   YIN
Feb. 13, 1926 - Feb. 1, 1927:   TIGER   YANG
Feb. 2, 1927 - Jan. 22, 1928:   RABBIT   YIN
Jan. 23, 1928 - Feb. 9, 1929:   DRAGON   YANG
Feb. 10, 1929 - Jan. 29, 1930: SNAKE   YIN
Jan. 30, 1930 - Feb. 16, 1931: HORSE   YANG
Feb. 17, 1931 - Feb. 5, 1932:   GOAT   YIN
Feb. 6, 1932 - Jan. 25, 1933:   MONKEY   YANG
Jan. 26, 1933 - Feb. 13, 1934: ROOSTER   YIN
Feb. 14, 1934 - Feb. 3, 1935:   DOG   YANG
Feb. 4, 1935 - Jan. 23, 1936:   PIG   YIN

Jan. 24, 1936 - Feb. 10, 1937: RAT   YANG
Feb. 11, 1937 - Jan. 30, 1938: OX   YIN
Jan. 31, 1938 - Feb. 18, 1939: TIGER   YANG
Feb. 19, 1939 - Feb. 7, 1940:   RABBIT   YIN
Feb. 8, 1940 - Jan. 26, 1941:   DRAGON   YANG
Jan. 27, 1941 - Feb. 14, 1942: SNAKE   YIN
Feb. 15, 1942 - Feb. 4, 1943:   HORSE   YANG
Feb. 5, 1943 - Jan. 24, 1944:   GOAT   YIN
Jan. 25, 1944 - Feb. 12, 1945: MONKEY   YANG

Feb. 13, 1945 - Feb. 1, 1946:	ROOSTER	YIN
Feb. 2, 1946 - Jan. 21, 1947:	DOG	YANG
Jan. 22, 1947 - Feb. 9, 1948:	PIG	YIN

Feb. 10, 1948 - Jan. 28, 1949:	RAT	YANG
Jan. 29, 1949 - Feb. 16, 1950:	OX	YIN
Feb. 17, 1950 - Feb. 5, 1951:	TIGER	YANG
Feb. 6, 1951 - Jan. 26, 1952:	RABBIT	YIN
Jan. 27, 1952 - Feb. 13, 1953:	DRAGON	YANG
Feb. 14, 1953 - Feb. 2, 1954:	SNAKE	YIN
Feb. 3, 1954 - Jan. 23, 1955:	HORSE	YANG
Jan. 24, 1955 - Feb. 11, 1956:	GOAT	YIN
Feb. 12, 1956 - Jan. 30, 1957:	MONKEY	YANG
Jan. 31, 1957 - Feb. 17, 1958:	ROOSTER	YIN
Feb. 18, 1958 - Feb. 7, 1959:	DOG	YANG
Feb. 8, 1959 - Jan. 27, 1960:	PIG	YIN

Jan. 28, 1960 - Feb. 14, 1961:	RAT	YANG
Feb. 15, 1961 - Feb. 4, 1962:	OX	YIN
Feb. 5, 1962 - Jan. 24, 1963:	TIGER	YANG
Jan. 25, 1963 - Feb. 12, 1964:	RABBIT	YIN

Feb. 13, 1964 - Feb. 1, 1965:   DRAGON   YANG
Feb. 2, 1965 - Jan. 20, 1966:   SNAKE   YIN
Jan. 21, 1966 - Feb. 8, 1967:   HORSE   YANG
Feb. 9, 1967 - Jan. 29, 1968:   GOAT   YIN
Jan. 30, 1968 - Feb. 16, 1969:   MONKEY   YANG
Feb. 17, 1969 - Feb. 5, 1970:   ROOSTER   YIN
Feb. 6, 1970 - Jan. 26, 1971:   DOG   YANG
Jan. 27, 1971 - Jan. 15, 1972:   PIG   YIN

Jan. 16, 1972 - Feb. 2, 1973:   RAT   YANG
Feb. 3, 1973 - Jan. 22, 1974:   OX   YIN
Jan. 23, 1974 - Feb. 10, 1975:   TIGER   YANG
Feb. 11, 1975 - Jan. 30, 1976:   RABBIT   YIN
Jan. 31, 1976 - Feb. 17, 1977:   DRAGON   YANG
Feb. 18, 1977 - Feb. 6, 1978:   SNAKE   YIN
Feb. 7, 1978 - Jan. 27, 1979:   HORSE   YANG
Jan. 28, 1979 - Feb. 15, 1980:   GOAT   YIN
Feb. 16, 1980 - Feb. 4, 1981:   MONKEY   YANG
Feb. 5, 1981 - Jan. 24, 1982:   ROOSTER   YIN
Jan. 25, 1982 - Feb. 12, 1983:   DOG   YANG
Feb. 13, 1983 - Feb. 1, 1984:   PIG   YIN
FEB 2-1984-   RAT   YANG

A BRIEF LOOK AT THE SIGNS

Hundreds of years ago, Oriental philosophers discovered something amazing: Human beings had personality traits that were similar to each other, based on the year they were born. They also realized that certain animals had characteristics that corresponded to those of mortal men and women.

In essence, this is our "animal nature."

We will delve more fully into a description of the love aspects of each sign later in the book. To whet your appetite for what is to come, here is a quick rundown of the signs.

THE RAT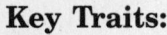

Key Traits:
Charming, sociable and restless.
Likes:
Diamonds, garnets, arts & crafts, interior design.
Dislikes:
Routine, being poor, watching the clock.
Love:
Romantic, attentive, passionate lovers – but they do tend to play the field.
Famous Rats:
Ursula Andress, Marlon Brando, Clark Gable, Richard Nixon, Burt Reynolds, George Washington.

THE OX

Key Traits:
Strong-willed, determined, ambitious, stubborn.
Likes:
Jade, emeralds, sports, gardening, music.
Dislikes:
Feeling insecure, playing games, making small-talk.
Love:
Loyal, caring, steadfast lovers.
Famous Oxen:
Warren Beatty, Bill Cosby, Jane Fonda, Angela Lansbury, Mary Tyler Moore, Napoleon.

THE TIGER

Key Traits:
Bold, adventurous, generous, impulsive.
Likes:
Rubies, diamonds, mystery novels, cooking.
Dislikes:
Compromise, bad manners, not being in charge.
Love:
Passionate, sincere, a true romantic.
Famous Tigers:
Tony Bennett, Garth Brooks, Tom Cruise, Marilyn Monroe, Demi Moore, Stevie Wonder.

THE RABBIT

DIAMONDS AND CRYSTALS

Key Traits:
Peace-loving, shrewd, prudent, perceptive.
Likes:
Pearls, crystals, emeralds, reading, hiking, gossip.
Dislikes:
Messy places, sudden change, too much physical contact.
Love:
Romantic, passionate, sensitive lovers.
Famous Rabbits:
Ingrid Bergman, Bob Hope, Whitney Houston, Jane Seymour, Tina Turner.

THE DRAGON

Key Traits:
Active, confident, honest, lucky.
Likes:
Opal, sapphire, astrology, dinosaurs.
Dislikes:
Being bullied, negativity, people who don't pull their weight.
Love:
Faithful, sincere and demanding.
Famous Dragons:
Bing Crosby, Neil Diamond, David Hasselhoff, Tom Jones, Al Pacino.

THE SNAKE

Key Traits:
Wise, thoughtful, guarded, slow-moving.
Likes:
Jasper, topaz, photography, painting.
Dislikes:
Noisy crowds, mistakes, being stood up.
Love:
Seductive, strongly sexed and possessive.
Famous Snakes:
Ann-Margret, Pierce Brosnan, Greta Garbo, Brooke Shields, Oprah Winfrey.

THE HORSE

Key Traits:
Active, alert, sociable, self-centered.
Likes:
Turquoise, topaz, athletics, theater, music.
Dislikes:
Being ignored, jealousy, loss of independence.
Love:
Passionate and faithful – when the right partner is found.
Famous Horses:
Kevin Costner, Clint Eastwood, Ella Fitzgerald, Paul McCartney, Barbra Streisand.

THE GOAT

Key Traits:
Creative, kind, easygoing, sensitive.
Likes:
Sapphire, jade, tennis, movies, clothes.
Dislikes:
Inefficiency, conflict, being alone.
Love:
Affectionate and caring.
Famous Goats:
Mel Gibson, Julio Iglesias, Mick Jagger, Barbara Walters, Bruce Willis.

THE MONKEY

Key Traits:
Versatile, charming, sociable, cunning.
Likes:
Crystal, aquamarine, word games, dancing.
Dislikes:
Being told to be quiet, being unpopular.
Love:
Captivating, but fickle.
Famous Monkeys:
Johnny Cash, Michael Douglas, Mia Farrow, Rod Stewart, Elizabeth Taylor.

THE ROOSTER

Key Traits:
Methodical, efficient, proud, candid.
Likes:
Diamonds, rubies, golf, singing, hiking.
Dislikes:
Bad manners, being teased, taking orders, dirty places.
Love:
Sincere, caring, loyal.
Famous Roosters:
Eric Clapton, Joan Collins, Gloria Estefan, Melanie Griffith, Dolly Parton.

THE DOG

Key Traits:
Honest, trusting, perceptive, cynical.
Likes:
Carnelian, jasper, gardening, crafts, cooking.
Dislikes:
Temper tantrums, disloyalty, hurt feelings.
Love:
Loyal.
Famous Dogs:
Cher, Sally Field, Michael Jackson, Elvis Presley, Sylvester Stallone.

THE PIG

Key Traits:
Sincere, sociable, hard-working, stubborn.
Likes:
Coral, lapis lazuli, shopping, dinner parties.
Dislikes:
Arguments, an empty wallet, an empty refrigerator, injustice.
Love:
Sensual and passionate.
Famous Pigs:
Julie Andrews, Fred Astaire, Hillary Clinton, Dudley Moore, Arnold Schwarzenegger.

THE RAT

YEARS
1912
1924
1936
1948
1960
1972
1984

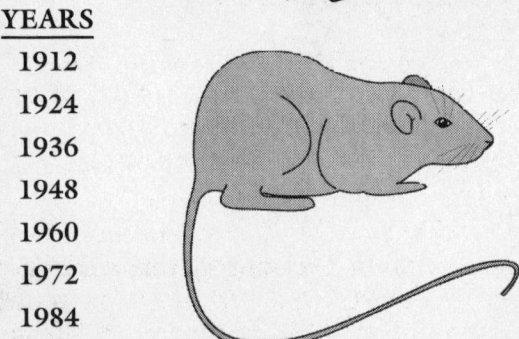

Unlike the Western concept of a rat, in Chinese culture Rats represent intelligent, captivating and loving people. They have a magnetism that easily attracts members of the opposite sex.

Male and female Rats are romantic and fall in love at the brush of a whisker. They prefer to mate for life and dislike being alone. Both male and female rats like to take the initiative, which can make for a lively relationship.

The Rat loves to party and appreciates the finer things in life. Improving his or her social level and standard of living is very important. This makes the Rat a hard worker.

Rats are thrifty and cautious about spending their hard-earned cash. However, a buying spree is a common release. So are whimsical purchases – especially when the Rat is buying something for a romantic partner.

鼠牛虎兔龍蛇馬羊猴鶏犬豬

IF YOU ARE A FEMALE RAT

*Y*OUR flirtatious nature is your greatest asset in a social situation. Since the Rat is a nocturnal creature, if you were born under this sign, you love the night life. Staying up until dawn is nothing out of the ordinary for you.

You have the uncanny ability to understand human nature, and you are able to put people at ease. Because of your perceptive nature, you will often be sought after for an opinion on spiritual, romantic or financial matters.

Whether you consider it a blessing or a curse, female Rats fall in love easily. They tumble tail over whiskers when someone catches their eye. In fact, Rats are happiest when they have a mate at their side.

One of the charming aspects of your personality is the tendency to indulge your children. You find it difficult to deny your little ones anything. And your kids are quick to learn that they can wrap mommy around their little fingers. This is something you must be aware of.

It is your nature to agonize over details, from the smallest to the largest. It's also part of your personality to become impatient with people who are slower than you are. And since Rats have such a sharp intellect, this is a part of your temperament that needs to be carefully monitored. You don't want to offend people and isolate yourself.

IF YOU LOVE A MALE RAT

Charm is a male Rat's biggest asset. He can enchant and seduce. But be aware that he will keep his ties to past lovers. He thinks nothing of picking up where he left off with an old flame. This can put a new relationship in jeopardy or cause friction and tension. This is part of his personality, and you either go with it or move on to another mate born under another sign.

The male Rat may appear to be quite sociable, but he guards his privacy. Don't expect him to open up to you quickly – or at all. There is a certain independence to his nature that will automatically exclude you. Don't think that means he doesn't love you.

In fact, Rats make wonderful fathers and are good family men. He will want a large family, and he will encourage his children to succeed. He will be a no-nonsense dad who sets high expectations for his offspring and helps them achieve their goals and dreams.

Be aware that behind the male Rat's suave, confident behavior is a strong, ambitious man. He will seek out what he wants and move with dogged determination until he gets it.

Although the male Rat may be a loving partner and outstanding father, he has his weak points. He may be crafty and manipulative. Driven by ambition and the need to better himself, the male Rat keeps himself busy, moving quickly from one project to another, each one bringing more success. His quick-witted nature means he will take risks, often with the money you have both set aside for a special purpose.

IF YOU ARE A MALE RAT

Chances are you stand out of the crowd and are quick to take advantage of that opportunity. You find it easy to gain the confidence of women, and you'll use it to your advantage.

You are intelligent, observant and completely at ease in a crowd. Your unique perception allows you to see all sides of an argument.

Work is your middle name, but you make a romantic lover. However, it is your tendency to date more than one lady at a time – until you settle down. Even then, when old flames appear, you may be tempted to play with fire. But be careful not to get burned and undo a strong and steady relationship for a fleeting whim.

You pride yourself on your passionate nature and there is a depth to your lovemaking that keeps a woman interested and content. This is a blessing in a long-term romance.

IF YOU LOVE A FEMALE RAT

The lady Rat will turn her home into her castle. She is domestic and supportive of your ambitions and goals. However, female Rats are involved in a variety of activities and often juggle many balls at once, so don't expect her to be waiting at home every night with dinner on the table. It may be that she'd love to provide the image of matrimonial bliss for you, but a host of other things need her attention – including work, the kids, special projects and volunteering.

Remember, the female Rat is a social creature who has many friends – all of whom vie for her attention, too.

Your Rat has a tendency to be a collector. She doesn't like waste and hates to throw things away. Be careful that your cozy love nest doesn't become a trash heap. When the closets and cupboards are full, take time together to throw some things away. You will both have to work hard to keep your home neat and clean, and not overflowing with junk.

She makes a steady and faithful spouse so be careful not to abuse her trust. And don't think you can fool her. She's quick-witted and intuitive. Don't count on her not knowing if you are finding somewhere else to nest now and then.

AWESOME UNIONS

Rat & Rat: Since both are romantic, passionate and share common goals, this is an ideal match. They value the sanctity of home, and Rat families will be close-knit. Resourceful and reliant, they make a devoted pair.

Rat & Ox: Although the Rat is more sociable than the Ox, these two signs mesh well in the romance department. With trust and respect, they support each other's strengths. Since each is mindful of his or her partner's character, together they can have a stable and secure relationship.

Rat & Dragon: These two lively, outgoing personalities get on well together. In love and marriage, this couple is ideally suited. They have many common interests, and they take pleasure in travel, raising a family and being romantic with each other. Physical attraction is a big plus in this winning combination.

Rat & Snake: The Snake is attracted to the Rat's outgoing charm, while the Rat is captivated by the Snake's seductive nature. Both are resourceful and bright; both enjoy the creature comforts the good life can provide. While the Snake takes it slow and the Rat jumps ahead, with a little effort this can be a blessed union.

Rat & Monkey: Outgoing, vivacious and social creatures, the Rat and the Monkey support and encourage each other. The Monkey appreciates the Rat's deftness in running a home and admires her organization. Likewise, the Rat admires the Monkey's social skills and enterprising nature. Together, they are devoted with mutual respect and love.

LOVE MATCHES

Great:
Dragon, Monkey, Rat, Ox, Snake
Just Average:
Pig, Tiger, Dog
Challenging:
Rabbit, Horse, Goat, Rooster

THE OX

YEARS
1913
1925
1937
1949
1961
1973
1985

Ox people are private and don't care a whole lot for socializing. Instead, they prefer a calm, quiet way of life. They move at a slow, steady pace – plowing through life – not venturing far from home.

If you are born under the sign of the Ox, you live an orderly existence. But because you are cautious, you may appear stubborn and unyielding.

However, you will do well at your chosen profession and can look forward to achievement in your field of endeavor. Moving at your own speed, independently of others, is your ideal. Being in business for yourself may be the best working situation since you are disciplined and ambitious. Harness on the yoke and you'll be on your way to success. This is especially true of women, who can combine home and business, giving them the best of both possible worlds.

鼠牛虎兔龍蛇馬羊猴鷄犬豬

IF YOU ARE A FEMALE OX

*Y*OUR home is your castle – a place where you can relax and be with your loved ones. Your greatest love is your family and the comfort of being in your own space, which you have decorated in a cozy, comfortable style.

Instead of partying and socializing like the Rat, you prefer gardening, reading, cooking and other quiet, reflective hobbies. You find serenity in nature and would prefer to live in the country, if possible. Dressing up is not your thing. Instead, you prefer simple clothing and little or no jewelry other than your wedding ring, of course.

Children are very important, and you are a nurturing and protective parent. You are busy from dawn to dusk, making sure your offspring and your mate are comfortable. Like the male Ox, you plow through the day with domestic chores, making sure everything is perfect.

You want to have children early and you delight in their accomplishments. As they grow up and spread their wings, you have a hard time letting them leave the nest. This is perfectly normal, especially for someone of your sign.

Organization is your middle name. You are practical and very much aware of your responsibilities and capabilities. Your down-to-earth nature makes you easygoing and agreeable. It seems as though you have energy to spare, and you need it with all the projects you have going.

IF YOU LOVE A MALE OX

Don't expect your Ox to shower you with words of love. Although he has a big heart, he doesn't like to express himself verbally. Save yourself a bundle of heartache and don't wait for him to say, "I love you." While he probably feels it, he simply cannot say it.

Also, know that he's not a social creature. If you love to go out and socialize, don't expect him to go. And if he does, don't expect him to have a good time. That's not his nature. He'd rather be home watching television or puttering around the house, fixing it up.

He is quiet and confident. His mind is sharp and his perseverance is steady. While he may appear calm on the outside, he is ambitious and will work hard to provide you and his family with all the necessities in life.

On the plus side, he thrives on a long-term, committed relationship. If you've hooked up with a male Ox, you're in for the long haul. He doesn't care for change. While he may seem to take forever making up his mind to settle down, once he does it will be "until death do you part." If you are lucky enough to have an Ox for a partner, you can trust him to be loyal and faithful.

Be aware, however, that he may become preoccupied with "doing his own thing" and may ignore you on occasion. Since his nature is fairly easygoing, he can be coaxed away from his projects and convinced to spend time with the family. But always allow him his own time and space.

You'll be glad to know, however, that he will defend those who are close to him if danger is nearby.

IF YOU ARE A MALE OX

You take a long time to make up your mind. However, once you do, you are patient and persistent — and will work toward your long-term goals. But on occasion, you tend to push too hard and don't listen to those around you. This is the stubborn streak that all Ox people have. For a successful relationship, you need to temper this tendency and accept the opinions of your life partner.

Being a workaholic is part of your nature. You can't help yourself. However, it would be best for everyone around you if you could ease up a bit. After all, just because you are born under this sign, doesn't mean you are a beast of burden.

At work, you are honest and conscientious. You are careful about your finances, investing wisely for the future.

But you do tend to be opinionated and inflexible. You don't like change, and you can be a poor sport when you lose. You lose your temper quickly, but luckily this happens only on rare occasions. It takes a conscious effort on your part not to be resentful when things don't go your way.

Slow and steady is the way you work and play. Luckily, your tenacity will get you to the finish line with style.

IF YOU LOVE A FEMALE OX

She may seem overly cautious, but that's OK. It will take her a long time to let you into her confidence. Instead of having a large social group, Ox females have one or two steady girlfriends with whom they share all their intimate secrets.

One difficulty with Ox women – and men, too – is they each like to have the final word. This can quickly lead to problems in a marriage. Sadly, too many Ox marriages fall apart when she insists on dominating the relationship. Remember, each side has to give in a marriage.

On the plus side, you'll find the female Ox is a loving, dedicated mate. She is supportive of her man and her children. She dresses simply and does not require an extravagant lifestyle. She delights in keeping her home clean and cozy – a place where you can put your feet up and relax.

Even though you may think she dotes on the kids too much, she makes a great mom. In the end, her patience and devotion to them pay off. You can be proud to watch them excel under her loving guidance.

AWESOME UNIONS

Ox & Snake: With quiet, reserved natures and thoughtful, reflective ways, the Ox and the Snake are a good match. Their strengths complement one another. Since they are on the same wavelength, the union is blessed with harmony. They make caring, responsible parents and tender, understanding lovers.

Ox & Rooster: Sexual attraction is the key factor that brings these two signs together. They work well together in the bedroom and in the boardroom. They make good business partners and are never bored with each other or with their life together. This sizzling combination is a prime example of how two signs can blend into a romantic whole.

Ox & Rabbit: Mutual admiration quickly turns to love, especially when trust is shared. While the Ox is more assertive than the Rabbit, the Rabbit delights in having a strong, goal-oriented partner. Since both are quiet and peace-loving, and since both value the harmony of a warm home and family life, they make an ideal pair.

LOVE MATCHES

Great:
Rat, Snake, Rooster, Rabbit
Just Average:
Ox, Monkey, Dog, Pig
Challenging:
Tiger, Horse, Goat, Dragon

THE TIGER

YEARS
1914
1926
1938
1950
1962
1974
1986

In the world of Chinese astrology, Tigers are considered a lucky sign. Perhaps this is due to their flamboyant and courageous nature.

Unimpressed with power or money, Tigers prefer a straightforward approach to life and love. They are powerful individuals with a wide range of interests. Their bold personality means they take many risks, but by following their convictions, they show honesty and integrity.

Tigers rely on their instinct, taking what they want. They make generous, honest friends and devoted partners once they have committed to a relationship.

In matters of the heart, Tigers are romantics – wanting to love and be loved. The nature of the beast means Tigers are restless. If you stop paying attention to your Tiger, he or she may wander. However, when the perfect mate is found, Tigers settle down with all the intentions of making it last forever.

IF YOU ARE A FEMALE TIGER

The female Tiger is a warm and friendly creature. She is outgoing and ambitious. Like her male counterpart, she is often asked to step into a position of authority and lead others. She is sleek and takes pride in her appearance. Her clothing will be fashionable and expensive.

The Tigress is brave and strong, but you are not immune to criticism. When it happens, you become depressed – but not for long. You bounce back quickly, ready for the next challenge. And you always land firmly on your feet.

Female Tigers are quick thinkers who react intelligently when danger is in the air. Unlike many people, you have long-range goals for which you strive with dignity and purpose.

Proud and independent, you know you can take care of yourself in any given situation. You sprint through each emergency, then take time to gather your wits and your strength. This does not make you any less romantic, it only makes you less needy.

When you look for love, it's because you want it. Your passion and energy shows through in the sensual excitement you arouse in your partner.

IF YOU LOVE A MALE TIGER

P*assion,* strength and courage describe the male Tiger. But give him his space or you'll drive him in search of other prey. He has an independent nature that cannot be dominated or tamed. That's what makes him what he is.

Like a real tiger, the Tiger sign is unpredictable. It would not be wise to assume he will act in any given way while under stress. He might surprise you. When backed into a corner, you may find him stubborn and fierce.

He is restless, always looking for an opportunity to move up the corporate ladder or into a romantic situation he feels is more advantageous. He certainly makes the most of a situation.

Tigers tend to be impatient and impulsive. In his desire to get to the top, he can be reckless or he can wear himself out trying.

Does he listen to advice? Not often. He thinks he has all the answers. And while he may have many, he will never admit that he doesn't know the others. Don't expect him to turn to you for advice. He'd rather slink into the bushes than admit he hasn't a clue. However, he's a quick learner, and it won't take long before he has a handle on the situation.

While Tigers have tremendous energy, they can easily burn themselves out. When your Tiger crawls into bed tired and anxious, he needs your soothing company to fortify himself for the next battle.

IF YOU ARE A MALE TIGER

You thrive on competition – especially on the job. You are a fast learner and like a challenge. That's why you won't stick long with any one career. The restless side of your nature will take over sooner or later.

Staying healthy is also part of your nature. When you feel stressed, take some time out to relax and enjoy life. Go on a vacation – get away for a while. Even a holiday with spills and thrills will energize your spirit – especially if you bask in the sun or explore the countryside.

Be wary of taking physical risks. It's in your personality to live on the edge, but danger lurks and you hate to be out of commission. Be cautious if you plan to take up rock climbing, snorkeling or bungee jumping!

From an early age, you don't like to be told what to do. Teachers, parents and girlfriends all have their place in your life, but you want to do things *your* way. This headstrong attitude will lead you into conflict with those close to you. When you settle down, allow your partner – especially if she is a Dragon or another Tiger – to come into the relationship on an equal footing. Otherwise, choose a less aggressive mate.

IF YOU LOVE A FEMALE TIGER

Remember, this woman is independent and strong-willed. She is also passionate and sexy. When she turns on the charm, be ready to keep up with her.

Use her vitality to energize the relationship. While she will try to dominate the partnership, she will also bring to it compassion, generosity and excitement. You have to let her take charge every now and then. If you go head-to-head, you're in for a good deal of grief.

On the plus side, the female Tiger protects her offspring with a vengeance. She is playful and affectionate, spoiling them with treats and attention. But don't cross her. She'll snarl with displeasure. There's no room for lack of respect, bad manners or rebellious behavior with this lady.

A Tigress will make a cozy nest but she also wants a career. She is good at whatever she does, so support her ambitions and give her plenty of room to make her dreams come true. The rewards will be many: financial stability, a happy partner, excitement in the relationship, passion and romance. You can have it all with a Tigress, if you don't dominate her. Let her do things her way – at least some of the time – and watch her blossom into a dynamic, vibrant woman.

AWESOME UNIONS

Tiger & Dog: Mutual respect and admiration are the key to this winning team. Often the Tiger and the Dog start as friends, learning about shared interests – which often spring from a common bond at work. While the Dog can be pessimistic, the optimistic Tiger makes a good antidote. Passion may be temperate, but it will be steady, with a loving and supportive marriage.

Tiger & Pig: A good sense of humor makes this combination delightful. Both are trusting and respectful of each other. With the extra added charge of physical attraction, these two can ignite the sparks of romance in no time at all. Together they have a wide circle of friends and enjoy socializing. The Tiger is the protecting force who benefits from the Pig's wise counsel.

Tiger & Rabbit: Although they are quite different, the Tiger and the Rabbit can find lasting love. Each draws from the other's strengths and blossoms within the relationship. Both are vivacious and enjoy an active life. They both like adventure, and travel will be part of their routine. But the Rabbit must allow the Tiger freedom, and the Tiger needs to respect the Rabbit's feelings for the union to flourish.

Tiger & Dragon: With passion running high, this can be a volatile combination. There will be romance – sparks flying – and never a dull moment. However, since both signs are charged with energy and since both are outspoken, compromise is the name of the marriage game. Romantic sizzle can fizzle unless a happy medium can be found.

LOVE MATCHES

Great:
Horse, Dog, Pig, Rabbit, Dragon

Just Average:
Tiger, Rooster, Rat

Challenging:
Goat, Monkey, Ox, Snake

THE RABBIT

YEARS
1915
1927
1939
1951
1963
1975
1987

Rabbits are generally quiet creatures who prefer to keep out of the spotlight. But this doesn't mean they are loners. In fact, rabbits get along very well with others, and rarely lack for friends or lovers. They enjoy parties and social events.

These emotional and sentimental people would never intentionally hurt someone else, but they are easily hurt by criticism or thoughtless treatment from others.

Rabbits make good business people since they are shrewd negotiators and excellent diplomats. Once a Rabbit settles on an occupation, he or she sticks with it, rather than hopping from one job to another.

Rabbits are blessed with good health and longevity. However, they may be prone to allergies or intestinal disorders. Regular exercise should be made part of any Rabbit's routine, since they tend toward sedentary careers.

IF YOU ARE A FEMALE RABBIT

If you were born under the sign of the Rabbit, you shun the limelight, preferring to remain in the background. That means spending time with your loved ones and the wide circle of friends you have. Although you are comfortable in a crowd, you are not a show-off.

Generally speaking, your attitude is one of contentment. You savor life and present a happy face to the world. Most important, you are a peace-loving person. You will do your utmost to avoid an unpleasant situation and will shy away from conflict.

Looking your best is important to you. The clothes you choose will be stylish, chic and sophisticated. Carrying yourself well gives you the confidence you need to feel good about yourself.

Your home is very important. The elegant surroundings you create for yourself and your family make you feel secure and untroubled. You like shades of green and your flair for decorating includes a varied collection of antiques and other interesting, unique items which you select carefully and thoughtfully.

Communication is an important part of what makes your relationships work. You plan carefully and you let your partner in on every detail. One of your best traits is that you don't keep secrets. Being upfront is what makes for a blissful union, especially if your partner is another Rabbit who also shares his feelings, plans, dreams and desires.

IF YOU LOVE A MALE RABBIT

Although he will not engage in an argument simply for argument's sake, he will defend you in a difficult situation. He will try to talk his way out of trouble, but if he can't, he'll plunge in with both fists flying.

He is methodical in his business dealings and has excellent judgment when it comes to negotiating. He will err on the side of caution, however, in order to avoid a confrontation.

The male Rabbit is prudent with his money. He will invest his earnings wisely and save for the future. In your later years, life should be relaxed and free from financial worries.

Settling down may take some time for the male Rabbit. He has a romantic and passionate nature, and he will want to play the field before picking a mate for life.

But once he stops fooling around and gets down to the business of raising a family, the male Rabbit will stop flirting with others. He will make a loyal and faithful spouse – in most cases. Of course, there will always be the renegade Rabbit who can't stop himself from hopping away from the nest. But, for the most part, the majority are true to their life partner.

Although the male Rabbit may appear aloof, he is sensual and loving under his cool exterior. He is romantic, yet realistic, and he is tuned in to the female side of his nature. He can empathize when you are feeling down, and you will find him a comfort when you need consolation.

IF YOU ARE A MALE RABBIT

Male Rabbits often find themselves in the position of judge, diplomat or negotiator. These occupations suit you well since you are not given to quick decisions. Instead, you think things through and come to a careful decision. You would also succeed as an attorney, administrator or teacher. However, you prefer a low-stress job, if possible.

Like the female Rabbit, you dress impeccably. You carry yourself with dignity and rarely raise your voice.

Women consider you charming and a good catch. Your intellect and your good taste will be appreciated by anybody you plan to be with for a long time.

While you may appear fussy at times, you find life pleasant and engaging. Stability is important and once you've had your flings, you will look forward to building a home and having a cozy future with the woman of your choice.

If you are lucky enough to settle down with a female Rabbit, you should be in for a long, prosperous and easygoing marriage. You both want the same things out of life, with harmony being of utmost importance.

IF YOU LOVE A FEMALE RABBIT

Don't ever worry that your female Rabbit won't look her best. She carries herself in style – as though she just stepped from the pages of a fashion magazine. She speaks softly – even when she is upset.

Her kind and gentle nature is an asset in any social situation.

Your Rabbit mate has a flair for decorating and she will make you a comfortable and cozy home. She likes antiques, paintings and expensive *objects d'art*. Don't expect your Rabbit to settle for anything but the best. She delights in entertaining and wants her home to make a good impression on others.

The world of art and music is very important to the Rabbit. She thrives on culture. But that doesn't mean she can't enjoy a good joke. She's got a great sense of humor that often helps bail her out of a sticky or stressful situation.

A deep, caring nature makes the female Rabbit a wonderful mother. She will provide a steady ear for her family's problems. Her nurturing will help each offspring through the childhood diseases with as little discomfort as possible.

As a lover, she is romantic and sensitive to the needs of her partner. Although she is strong, she may be prone to mood swings. When her feelings are hurt, she will cry easily. However, with kind words and a little affection, all will be put right again.

AWESOME UNIONS

Rabbit & Rabbit: This easygoing combination between two mild-mannered people is bound to succeed. Living a high lifestyle and avoiding conflict are the two most important parts to this union. They enjoy conversation, fine things and have a mutual respect in the romance department. With everything going for them, two Rabbits make an elegant and loving team.

Rabbit & Goat: Shared interest and trust make this a winning duo. Neither likes friction or stress. Both want a comfortable home that provides a refuge from the wear and tear of life. Affection, loyalty and love bring out the best in their marriage.

Rabbit & Pig: Both are warm, happy and love the home – especially if it's in the country. These two peaceful signs are harmonious, respectful and content with each other. While passion won't burn up the bed, there is a caring and sharing that make this pair a good bet for a long-term relationship.

Rabbit & Ox: While the Ox tends to be more assertive than the more placid Rabbit, domestic bliss is possible. The Rabbit likes the protection the Ox offers, and the Ox thrives on the support the Rabbit gives. They both appreciate the finer things in life, including reading, theater and the arts. While the Ox may not like to socialize as much as his mate, with a little give-and-take this union can thrive.

LOVE MATCHES

Great:
Rabbit, Goat, Pig, Ox, Tiger

Just Average:
Dragon, Horse, Snake, Dog

Challenging:
Rat, Monkey, Rooster

THE DRAGON

YEARS
1916
1928
1940
1952
1964
1976
1988

Dragons are amazing folks – flamboyant, vibrant and filled with energy. They inspire and surprise others and thrive on drawing attention to themselves. They are born achievers and won't let anything, or anyone, stand in their way.

Courage, leadership and impatience are three of the Dragon's principal traits. They thrive on new challenges and are constantly setting new, loftier goals. However, they sometimes get carried away by their own intensity, and mistakes can happen. But Dragons recover quickly and are then off to the next task. They are admired by their peers for being fair, but they won't tolerate hypocrisy.

Dragons shy away from marriage and commitment. They relish their independence and feel shackled by the bonds of matrimony. However, if and when they do settle down, they remain loyal and faithful lovers.

IF YOU ARE A FEMALE DRAGON

Women born under the sign of the Dragon are filled with boundless energy and drive. They can go from dawn to dusk and still look refreshed and radiant at the end of a long day.

Dragons are inventive and original. If you were born under this sign, you will attract many people of the opposite sex. You are warm and charming, and men will automatically be drawn to your impulsive and outgoing nature. But they may soon be disappointed to learn that you don't need them as much as they need you.

You are a trendy, elegant extrovert with a dazzling personality. In fact, your tastes border on the extreme. You love to be noticed and admired, and you do whatever it takes to gain the attention and admiration of everyone you meet.

Independence is the name of your game, even though you fall in love easily. While you would like a steady partner, you are in no hurry to settle down. The world offers too many opportunities for committing quickly to a steady relationship.

You're a wonderful hostess and love to entertain. Part of the reason is that you love showing off your house and your latest collection of unique and bizarre *objects d'art*. That's OK. You're proud of your Dragon's den and love it when people comment on what you've done.

Children are nice – for other people or later in life. Having a brood of your own is not a top priority. Parenting does not come naturally to you, but once you have a few, you will lavish them with toys and games and love.

IF YOU LOVE A MALE DRAGON

Show-off is his middle name. He is a free spirit who hates to conform. He does things his way or no way. He's also an egotist who doesn't know the meaning of the word modesty.

Male Dragons are blessed with handsome faces and flamboyant personalities. Women will flock to them in social situations, and they thrive on the attention. But women will be disappointed to learn that he is simply toying with their affections. He can be a fickle creature who uses women, then discards them like old shoes.

A male Dragon may drive you crazy with his risk-taking – especially when it comes to money. It's not unusual for him to invest everything in a get-rich-quick scheme or what may appear to be a rock-solid investment. However, even if he loses his shirt in the venture, he'll start all over from scratch, rebuilding his fortune. Don't expect financial stability in your old age if you are with a male Dragon. It will be touch-and-go all the way through life.

Dragons are solitary individuals at heart. It will take a long time to break through his thick armor. For, in reality, he needs no close bonds to be happy.

One discouraging aspect of a Dragon's behavior is his need to dominate. He doesn't like taking advice and is quick to respond with put-downs – even to those he loves. He can be insensitive, but his irresistible charm overrides any bad habits and nasty traits.

IF YOU ARE A MALE DRAGON

Rules and restrictions were made for others, not you. You hate being told what to do. Since you run on high-energy octane, stress is the natural result and something you must learn to live with. Tension headaches, depression and high blood pressure are the price you pay for burning the candle at both ends.

On the other hand, your creativity is in much demand. But beware of jobs that can become routine. You'll soon hate any job that is the same every day.

When you do take a break from work, you won't join all the other tourists at the same old popular vacation spot. You want an out-of-the-way place where there are spills and thrills galore. Rock climbing, skiing and white-water rafting are the sports you find exhilarating.

Chances are you love being a bachelor and it suits you. Playing the field is more fun than settling down. And since you love being the center of attention, not having a spouse allows you all the freedom you could desire.

IF YOU LOVE A FEMALE DRAGON

Female Dragons do not thrive on domesticity. While she will want a large, imposing home, she won't spend much time there. Instead, she will be out in the world making her mark on society or in the business arena.

Spending money is one of the female Dragon's greatest pastimes. Since she likes to look good, her wardrobe will be trendy and expensive. She won't want to scrimp and will always buy the best that she can afford.

Of all the signs the Dragon is the most likely to be a gambler, especially the female Dragon. For the most part, she will usually be lucky, for she was born under a sign of good fortune. However, she must be careful not to be too reckless with her finances or take advantage of her good fortune.

The lady Dragon is constantly on the go and her enthusiasm and energy are infectious. She is always involved with a project or a game plan. Don't expect her to sit around waiting for you to decide what to do and make up your mind. She wants what she wants when she wants it. In fact, you may have a hard time getting her to settle down at the end of the day – or even permanently.

If you are able to persuade her to settle down, she wants to be the boss. While she will support your efforts and projects, she doesn't have a large capacity for understanding your problems. She can be stubborn and intolerant, but she works hard and loves deeply.

AWESOME UNIONS

Dragon & Rat: Both of these signs are social creatures with quick minds and an endless supply of energy. The easygoing Rat admires the dynamic Dragon, and the Dragon appreciates the empathy of the less outgoing Rat. Add the sensual nature of each, physical attraction and mental harmony, and this winning duo can't lose.

Dragon & Monkey: This social-minded pair enjoys each other's company. They provide a common support and trust, which makes them good business partners. With plenty of energy and enthusiasm, they will have a large circle of friends, but they will take time to please each other in private.

Dragon & Tiger: These two signs make sweet music together. It's a lusty merger with lots of passion and excitement. Traveling and socializing play a large part in their union. And while each wants a certain amount of independence, a happy medium can be reached with compromise and communication.

LOVE MATCHES

Great:
Rat, Monkey, Tiger
Just Average:
Snake, Horse, Pig, Rooster
Challenging:
Ox, Goat, Dog, Rabbit, Dragon

THE SNAKE

YEARS
1917
1929
1941
1953
1965
1977
1989

Snakes are charming, sophisticated and sexy – in a subtle way. They are private people and deep thinkers. It takes them a while to decide what they want, but when they know, they move toward their goals with ease.

Snakes are intelligent and successful without being pushy or overly aggressive. They are interested in many subjects – especially psychic matters. They are secretive and rarely let anyone know their private thoughts. While they can be social, they also need to be left alone.

The wisdom of Snakes is often sought by others. They make excellent mediators and judges with their careful analysis of any situation. Hard physical labor is not in the cards for Snakes. They prefer intellectual challenges, instead.

In the love department, Snakes are very choosy and take their time picking a mate. However, they are seductive, sultry and possessive.

IF YOU ARE A FEMALE SNAKE

*Y*ou are bewitching and beguiling, and many an unsuspecting male will be entranced by your perceptive mind and cool, sophisticated demeanor.

Dressing well is important to you, and you pay close attention to details of hair, nails and makeup. You feel your best after a visit to the salon, where you can relax and energize your spirit. The lady Snake has that certain something, a quiet sex appeal, that men find hard to resist.

When it comes to love, you may find that your first long-term relationship won't work out, but that won't stop you from finding another mate. Along the way, you accumulate children from your different unions. While you use humor to keep your kids in line, you find discipline difficult to administer. You'd rather go to the kitchen and make an elaborate meal than lay down the law.

When you are alone with your man, you become as sensuous as a serpent, steeling him with your steady gaze and seducing him in no time. He is your love slave and you have complete control – unless you are with a Dragon or another Snake.

IF YOU LOVE A MALE SNAKE

*C*ommunication is not his strong point, so don't expect him to verbalize his feelings. But he's a charmer, slithering his way into your heart before you know what's happened.

Beware, however, for he is something of a Don Juan and never lacks for sweethearts. His charm is irresistible – and not only to you. He cannot help himself when women throw themselves in his path. While he may appear to hold you at arm's length, once he has selected his mate, he will be quite possessive.

Socializing is not his thing. Male snakes are solitary creatures. They don't make friends easily and they avoid gatherings filled with small talk. To worm your way into his heart will take perseverance and an investment of time and energy. Take him on a weekend getaway to a quiet place. Once you have him alone, let him relax and enjoy the surroundings before trying to get close. Allow him to make the first move. If he feels he's backed into a corner, he'll slither away.

In any union, Snakes become surly if they are double-crossed. If you are in a relationship with a Snake, be upfront, open and honest. But don't be surprised if he keeps you guessing as to his intentions. Intrigue is part of his nature, and he plays his cards close to his chest in the love department.

The Snake wants his home to be pleasing, for it is the one place he can relax and unwind. He may be called a couch potato, but he doesn't care. Give him a few hours of peace and quiet and he'll soon be recharged.

IF YOU ARE A MALE SNAKE

Your ability to concentrate on a given task is inspiring to others. You have the ability to cut through the nonsense and get to the heart of the problem.

While nobody could call you lazy, doing nothing is one of your greatest pleasures. When vacation time rolls around, you won't be found making elaborate plans. Swinging in a hammock or lying on a sunny beach are the ultimate choices.

It's not unusual for you to have several marriages in your lifetime – as well as many children. That means a large and diverse family and many obligations. While you are devoted to your offspring, it is difficult to handle the noise and energy they produce, since peace and quiet are vital to your well-being. You would rather leave the discipline to your partner while you slide into a cozy corner and curl up with a good book.

Male Snakes are complex beings. It will take a while for you to decide what you want to do with your life. Once the goal is set, you make your way to that destination with a steady pace. You are good with finances, and you and your mate can look forward to retirement in style.

Wise and alert, you are also refined and gentle. You trust yourself to make sound judgments in business and in love. And if your choices don't work out, instead of agonizing, you move on with panache and confidence.

IF YOU LOVE A FEMALE SNAKE

Her appearance is impeccable, her manner refined. She appears interested and friendly, but she is secretly analyzing every move you make and every word you speak.

Female Snakes need plenty of space and alone-time. She will not be comfortable in noisy, bustling settings.

It will frazzle her nerves and make her unhappy and stressed out.

While the female Snake is a hard-worker, taking naps to revitalize her energy is part of her daily routine. She needs the time to recharge and relax. Stress is an ordeal that should be avoided at all costs.

If you want to please her, rent a villa on the ocean or a hilltop cabin and let her commune with nature. To enter her realm of spiritual awareness, join her on a retreat deep in the woods. There, you will learn more about your lady love than you ever could at home.

In love, you'll find female Snakes sleek and sensual. She will bewitch you with her sexy charm, and you will be overwhelmed with her intense passion.

Men should never assume that you will be the one. Female Snakes are very choosy in their selection of men. You will only be considered if you are good-looking, hard-working, quick-witted, refined, clever and have a sense of humor. Her remote yet alluring manner will keep you guessing – which adds to the excitement. You'll never know if she will coil around you or slither away.

AWESOME UNIONS

Snake & Ox: With both ambitious minds on the same wavelength, a partnership will flourish. The Ox's tenacity and the Snake's quick mind make this a good union. But in marriage, both are quiet and placid. Neither is a socializer, and home is very important for revitalizing the spirit. The Ox makes a good disciplinarian, which suits the Snake's less aggressive nature. Both find communing with nature beneficial. This tranquility carries over into sensual and caring pleasures in the bedroom.

Snake & Goat: Calm and easygoing, these two can quickly move from being friends to lovers. They feel comfortable with each other since neither pretends to be someone else. Both enjoy nature. The Goat is entranced by the Snake's insight, and the Snake is delighted with the Goat's artistic nature. There is love and harmony in the union.

Snake & Rooster: Mutual admiration makes this a good match. Both are intellectual and ambitious, but in a relaxed way. The Rooster's devotion to the home and children is admired by the Snake. And the Snake finds the Rooster's loyalty endearing. The Rooster's fussiness and the Snake's secretive nature challenge this match, but they can be overcome.

Snake & Dog: While there may not be an initial attraction, in the long run this combination can be a great success since there is a deep loyalty. The Snake is ambitious, and the Dog values the security that success can bring. While the Dog can be stubborn and moody, the Snake is willing to allow plenty of space. The Dog draws comfort from the Snake's quiet, calm, caring nature.

LOVE MATCHES

Great:
Ox, Goat, Rooster, Dog, Snake

Just Average:
Rat, Rabbit, Dragon

Challenging:
Tiger, Monkey, Pig, Horse

THE HORSE

YEARS
1918
1930
1942
1954
1966
1978
1990

HORSES are lively, straightforward, quick-witted and elegant. They enjoy a challenge, but they will gallop away if they feel dominated. Horses like new things, and their adventurous spirit means they live life to the fullest. They don't stay around long if what they are doing seems pointless.

Horses are an outgoing breed who make friends easily – and for a lifetime. You love the nightlife and socializing and are never short of invitations or dates. Your quick sense of humor and easygoing attitude attract people to you like flies.

Horse people fall in love all the time. Every relationship seems to be perfect, at first. They are passionate and faithful – and willing to risk everything for love. Their first few relationships probably won't last long, but Horses have the great ability to learn from past mistakes. When you find the right partner, it will last forever.

IF YOU ARE A FEMALE HORSE

Those born under the sign of the Horse are bursting with enthusiasm and energy. You are the life of the party, holding everyone's attention with your lively conversation. You come late, kick up a storm, then sprint for greener pastures, leaving those in your wake desperate for more.

Adaptable and imaginative, you are a persuasive speaker and are often called upon to make speeches for local civic groups and school meetings. Your good sense of humor makes you a popular guest at any gathering.

While you like socializing, home is the place you love to be, especially when surrounded by family and friends. Your decor is warm and inviting and you try hard to make everyone comfortable. While you enjoy handiwork, such as crafts and painting, you have little patience for household chores.

Looking good is important, and your clothes are chosen carefully. They are not expensive, but they are flattering. Colorful hues and bright florals look best on you. You attract much attention because you carry yourself with dignity and poise.

Falling in love is easy for you – perhaps too easy. You throw caution to the wind when it comes to romance. And when you are in love, it's a deep, long-lasting love. You are deeply loyal and you give one hundred percent of yourself to your mate. If it doesn't work out, you can be devastated. Luckily, your nature doesn't allow you to wallow in self-pity. You spring back into action in no time at all.

IF YOU LOVE A MALE HORSE

The Horse has a keen mind and a quick spirit. He's impulsive and erratic. When the time is right, he makes a loyal mate, but beforehand, he prefers to roam. Independence and freedom are top priorities in his relationships. This may not go over well with you, but he will be honest about it.

On the plus side, he is likeable and not overly impressed with his own talents. He is a caring partner without being bossy or boastful. Although there will be occasions when he will lose his temper, it won't happen often. Afterward, he is remorseful and repentant. An apology should be forthcoming, and you'll forgive him easily, since his zest for life means you cannot stay mad for long.

This man loves to travel. Don't be surprised if he comes home one evening and tells you to pack a suitcase. He likes the feel of the wind in his hair and finds roughing it in a national park a perfect vacation. He's not inclined to make reservations at a luxury hotel, so don't expect a holiday in high style.

When it comes to kids, he's a no-nonsense guy. He's not going to be gushy and sentimental with his offspring. He will expect them to be self-sufficient, the way he is. In the early years, he will nurture this independence. As they grow older, he'll expect them to go out on their own, just as he did.

The male Horse is charming and hard to resist. He'll fall in love quickly, but he may later regret his haste. For a stable relationship with a Horse, wait until he's older before trying to rope him in. By then, he should know what he wants.

IF YOU ARE A MALE HORSE

You are dependable and honest. People enjoy being around you and look to you as a leader. But you can be impatient and reckless if you are not careful.

Boundless energy makes you a gifted worker. The world is open to your talents, from journalism to professional sports. There is nothing you cannot do – except the mundane. But you tend to jump from one occupation to another – sometimes quitting a job before you have secured another. This doesn't bother you, though; you know there is something better waiting for you.

You enjoy being around people, especially a small group of select friends, with whom you can relax and be yourself. People of both sexes gravitate toward you, and women find you hard to resist. Some only want a friendship, but most want much more.

It will take you a while to settle down. Life is far too entertaining to get married early. In fact, if you do marry early, it will probably be a mistake. It will take you some time to discover which path you wish to pursue. Being burdened with a spouse and family at a young age will make you even more restless. Take your time. That way, when you select a partner for life, you will pick wisely.

IF YOU LOVE A FEMALE HORSE

Female Horses are loyal to their friends, co-workers and especially their partners. They are self-reliant and this independent nature makes them a natural helpmate. A female Horse will stick by your side, giving endless love and support.

Money is not of utmost importance to the female Horse. If you have it, she'll spend it. But when finances are low, she can pull in the belt and stick to a budget.

She is drawn to a profession with words – as a language interpreter, tour guide, writer, poet, librarian or teacher. Her gifts are her quick mind and her ability to pick up new skills.

Housework is not her strong point so you'll have to lend a hand if you want a clean home. She is distracted easily and will leave a project unfinished as she turns her attention to something new.

Once a family is in the picture, the female Horse has the unique ability to juggle home, career, spouse and children with amazing calmness. She will instill self-reliance in her offspring so she can continue with her career. Don't expect her to give up everything for the kids. Her own needs and desires are on an equal par with theirs – and yours.

AWESOME UNIONS

Horse & Tiger: This dynamic duo makes sparks fly. They are both willing to take a risk, especially when it comes to romance. Their bold, enterprising and hard-working temperaments go hand-in-hand with sensuality – making this a match that can endure the strains of matrimony. Each needs independence, and each is willing to give the other the space he or she needs to grow and flourish. Although both signs can be stubborn, opinionated and headstrong, they can ride out any differences by keeping the channels of communication open.

Horse & Goat: This union starts off as good friends, but gathers steam as time goes by. The ties become deeper and richer as more and more intimacy is shared. Although the personalities of the Horse and Goat are quite different, they each lend support to the other. Both are social creatures, and they have many interests in common. The Horse is strong and the Goat is resourceful. They listen to each other and respect one another's ideas. As romance grows, so does the passion they share.

Horse & Dog: Stability is what this team has going for it. With trust and loyalty as the core of the relationship, this pair can't go wrong. The Horse values the Dog's love and affection. The Dog draws strength from the Horse, especially when things aren't going well. Thus, helping and supporting each other, they can make a marriage thrive.

LOVE MATCHES

Great:
Tiger, Goat, Dog
Just Average:
Dragon, Rooster, Rabbit, Horse
Challenging:
Rat, Ox, Monkey, Pig, Snake

THE GOAT

YEARS
1919
1931
1943
1955
1967
1979
1991

鼠牛虎兔龍蛇馬羊猴鶏犬豬

These intelligent creatures don't like to be rushed or pressured into anything, and that includes love. They can be moody and sullen, yet they are also loving, sensitive and talented. Highly artistic and imaginative, they often appear to be living in their own world.

Goats are so easygoing, yet they are inclined to worry about everything under the sun and need constant reassurance. Shy and sympathetic to others, Goats are easily intimated and become very upset by confrontations.

While Goats love being in the company of others, they may appear reserved and a bit aloof on first meeting. They have no desire to stand in the spotlight, and prefer to be influential in their own quiet way.

With their affectionate and caring nature, Goats make the perfect domestic partner. What they want most in life is a loving partner and comfortable home.

IF YOU ARE A FEMALE GOAT

Go with the flow is your motto. You are idealistic and more than a little impractical. You are happiest when you are at home with your creative projects. Your ideal is peace and quiet with few distractions and no stress.

Compassion for others goes hand-in-hand with your creativity. Volunteer work is important to your sense of self. Your kind, gentle nature is appreciated by others, especially those less fortunate. But be careful not to allow others to take advantage of your giving spirit. You tend to let others take control of your life, which can be a dangerous thing. Beware of becoming too dependent on your partner.

Your home will be lovingly decorated with down-to-earth furnishings. Walking into your home puts a visitor immediately at ease, and you have the satisfaction of knowing it didn't cost a fortune.

Children light up your life and you are a natural-born mother. And while you form close attachments with them, it is easy for you to become possessive and smother them with affection. Having your extended family around, especially your parents, is also very important to you. Instilling proper manners and respect for their elders is something you do for your children from the very beginning.

An intimate and loving union is essential for your well-being and peace of mind. Since you are family-oriented, you feel incomplete if you are alone. Love is waiting for you and when you find it, the union will be harmonious and long-lasting.

IF YOU LOVE A MALE GOAT

You may find the male Goat is a bit on the fussy side. While he will be gentle and kind, he can also be moody and insecure. But these are his only major shortcomings.

Because he gravitates toward the arts, financial success and the acquisition of material goods are not of great importance. Instead, he would rather write, play music, act or paint.

Time has little meaning for Goats of either gender. Don't be surprised if he's late for appointments or dates. Once he's involved in a project, he becomes single-minded, blocking out everything else.

One thing is certain, he won't be climbing up the corporate ladder. He's not a born leader and he doesn't relish that role in any case. So while his paycheck won't be huge, he'll have more time to spend with his family.

If you've settled down with a male Goat, you are a lucky lady. He is a loving and responsible parent who enjoys the company of his children. You can count on this dad to spend many hours playing with the kids.

Like females born under this sign, male Goats don't spill their secrets freely. His list of acquaintances is long, but his list of solid friends is short. It will take a long time before he'll let you know who he really is.

When you find the Goat of your dreams, he will be romantic, soft-hearted, gentle and compassionate. This is not a sign of weakness. It's simply his character traits coming through. He might not light rockets under the bed, but he will be a caring and steadfast partner.

IF YOU ARE A MALE GOAT

A job in a stressful environment is not for you. You prefer quiet occupations such as writing, architecture and the arts.

It's in your nature to be a follower. So when vacation time rolls around, you'll look for a group tour or a place like Club Med where you can be around others. You are not looking for thrills and spills. Instead, you like to socialize with a small party while you see distant lands.

You don't care for rules and regulations, but you don't like confrontations, either. So when you come across a situation that bothers you, you will do things your own way – quietly. You're not looking to attract attention to yourself, you just want to get the job done. The only business quality that's lacking in your personality is organization.

You find it difficult to express yourself in a romantic situation. Even when you feel love, you have difficulty expressing yourself. But any woman you want to settle down with will be able to see your sensitive and caring side, even if the words are not spoken.

IF YOU LOVE A FEMALE GOAT

The lady Goat loves to stay at home with her children and her husband. The Goat makes an ideal lover and wife for any male who wants to settle down to a life of comfort and tranquility. Of course, if you like to travel and socialize, stay away from the female Goat – because the two of you will not mix.

She may be shy and reserved upon first meeting. Give her time and she'll open up. Female Goats change their minds quickly and often. It may throw you for a loop on occasion, but it's simply her capricious nature, not anything you've done.

You will always be proud to have a female Goat at your side. She is a modest and unpretentious helpmate who supports your career and nourishes your soul.

AWESOME UNIONS

Goat & Rabbit: The placid nature of these two signs makes it a natural pairing. They trust and respect one another, which helps them work together as a business team. Since the Goat needs a prod now and then, the Rabbit is the perfect motivator. Neither the Goat nor the Rabbit care for conflict, which means that they should get along without rancor. And since both are deeply committed to the arts, they have much in common.

Goat & Horse: Although the Horse is more outgoing and lively than the Goat, their personalities are very compatible. They often start as good friends and move into a romantic relationship later in life. Both enjoy the company of others, yet they each like to be alone for some romantic time together. The strength of the Horse complements the domestic disposition of the Goat, making this an excellent match.

Goat & Pig: The robust, fun-loving nature of the Pig works well with the home-loving character of the Goat. They balance each other. In a business sense, the Pig takes the Goat's creative ideas and makes them marketable. It is a dynamic way of making money. In romance, both are sensual and physically stimulated by the other. They can produce a harmonious, compatible, fulfilling union.

Goat & Goat: With a love of the arts and no one to dominate the relationship, how can this pair lose? The attraction of two Goats is very strong. They know how to enjoy themselves in the kitchen with tasty food and exotic wines. And when they are not being stubborn or impulsive, they get on well together, especially in bed.

Great:
Rabbit, Horse, Pig, Goat
Just Average:
Snake, Monkey, Dragon
Challenging:
Rat, Ox, Rooster, Dog, Tiger

THE MONKEY

YEARS
1920
1932
1944
1956
1968
1980
1992

These bright, witty creatures adapt easily to any situation. They love to socialize and easily capture the attention of others with their zany antics. Monkeys excel in linguistics and are regular chatterboxes, making them the life of the party. This gift of gab comes in useful when they need to talk themselves out of trouble – something that occurs frequently.

They are restless animals, however, and find it hard to settle down to a routine. If their progress in completing a task is taking too long, they lose interest and abandon the goal.

Monkeys can also be crafty, using any trick in the book to get what they want. In financial matters, the Monkey is shrewd and clever, profiting from any scheme.

When in love, they are captivating, but fickle – and sometimes find it difficult to remain true to one partner.

IF YOU ARE A FEMALE MONKEY

Bright and quick-thinking, you excel in anything you put your mind to – and you have a great time during the process. There is nothing you won't try once. The world is a challenge and you are up to the task.

You pride yourself on being able to find a shortcut to the finish line, and doing the job in half the time is your trademark. You have a way with money and your quick tongue makes you an excellent salesperson. A career in real estate or marketing is only overshadowed by acting, writing and handicrafts.

When you settle down to raise your family – something you definitely want – you aren't willing to sacrifice your active social life. The first thing you'll do is find a few qualified babysitters so you can go out on the town whenever you want. When you are home though, you love every second you spend with your kids. And they will pick up on your sense of humor and your non-judgmental way of dealing with their own problems.

When it comes to love, you can be a downright flirt. Nothing pleases you more than having men swoon at your feet. It's this frisky side of your character that men find irresistible. But you may not be honest in telling them how you feel.

IF YOU LOVE A MALE MONKEY

This clever two-stepper can dance rings around everyone, including his mate. Male Monkeys are tricksters who are hard to pin down to a committed relationship. But he is charming and funny and always has a joke or humorous story up his sleeve.

You'll never be bored around a Monkey. And even though he may dangle your affection on a string, it's hard to stay mad at him.

But beware, the male Monkey bores easily. He can become restless at the drop of a hat. When your Monkey needs to get away from it all, don't expect him to head for the hills or the solitude of a cabin in the woods. He needs to be around people and craves socializing and the night life.

The male Monkey will toy with you for a while, teasing and amusing you with his brilliant mind. But he tends to keep his true feelings bottled up inside. He can be secretive and evasive, which may work against him, if he loses the lady he truly loves. However, once he settles down, he is a passionate and intense lover.

IF YOU ARE A MALE MONKEY

You have plenty of good friends and never lack for company – male or female. Since you're such a social creature, you hate being sick. Life is too short to be out of commission. So you push yourself to the limit, physically and mentally. It might be a healthy idea to slow down a little, but it's difficult for you to do.

Live for the moment is your philosophy. Putting money away for a rainy day takes a back seat to fun. While you can make a decent living, you spend what you earn.

You prefer to play the field when it comes to love. You have the tendency to be promiscuous, but having several lovers at one time is very risky these days, so beware. When it comes to love and dating, your cunning ways will soon reveal themselves, for you think nothing of lying to save your romantic hide. You use humor to deflect the anger of your female partners. And while it's fun for you to play the field, this dangerous practice has a way of backfiring when you least expect it.

Looking good is important, especially your hair. Some may find this tendency to preen a streak of vanity. However, it is within your character to want to appear your best.

Growing old is not something you look forward to. That's why you work so hard to retain your youthful spirit. Keeping in shape will help fend off the ills encountered later in life.

IF YOU LOVE A FEMALE MONKEY

This resourceful lady is a real gem. With a sense of humor and an imagination that runs wild, she's always game for anything. But she can be a mischievous prankster.

You may think your female Monkey is just plain

nosy, but it's just her inquisitive nature. She needs to know the answers to endless questions.

She prefers city living to country dwelling. And while she likes being entertained, if no parties or social events are going on, she can sit in the mall and watch people for hours on end. But put her in a boring movie, concert or play and she'll get up and walk out.

Don't expect your female Monkey to sit home quietly and watch television. If she's home, the telephone is in her hand and she's gabbing away to her friends. This is an important part of her life and she needs to express herself constantly. Think of it as monkey chatter.

Besides her wonderful sense of humor, one of the best traits of female Monkeys is that they retain their youthful zest for life. They enjoy being around young people and feel no generation gap. If you remain open-minded, it can keep you feeling young, too.

AWESOME UNIONS

Monkey & Monkey: Monkeys like to have a good time, which makes them well-suited for each other. Both are resourceful and quick problem-solvers. Although they may try to outdo each other, if two Monkeys can combine their strengths, they will make a great money-making team. This rapport can be transferred easily to a romance, and lovemaking will be fun, fun, fun.

Monkey & Rat: These lively, sociable signs get on well together. The Rat has the drive and the Monkey has a great sense of humor and an inquisitive mind. Together they inspire one another. As a couple, they have mutual love and respect. Their home is filled with good vibrations and lots of affection.

Monkey & Dragon: Although the Dragon is more flamboyant, both enjoy socializing and traveling. The ability to understand each another makes this a formula for success. Both have the zest to undertake a project and carry it through to completion. In private, passion prevails with these lively signs. Anything goes in the love and romance department – the wilder – the better.

Great:
Monkey, Rat, Dragon
Neutral:
Snake, Goat, Dog, Pig
Challenging:
Rabbit, Rooster, Horse, Tiger, Ox

THE ROOSTER

YEARS
1921
1933
1945
1957
1969
1981
1993

Up early and always alert, Roosters make the most of each and every day. They may seem fussy with their constant preening, but Roosters have an eye for detail, and they like to do things the right way.

With a remarkable memory, Roosters know a little bit about everything. If there's a debate raging, a Rooster will jump into the ring, astounding nearby listeners. They are fascinating and entertaining people to be around.

Like the Dragon, the Rooster appears flamboyant. There is a thin line between the Rooster's confident, self-assured manner and his or her vanity.

On the down side, Roosters are rather picky and particular. They also may be domineering and difficult to live with. But once a Rooster is settled down with the partner of their choice, they will be a devoted partner and a helpful parent.

鼠牛虎兔龍蛇馬羊猴雞犬豬

IF YOU ARE A FEMALE ROOSTER

You are careful and conscientious in everything you do. You set high standards for yourself and for others. Truth is your middle name and you find it difficult to lie, even when it would spare someone's feelings.

Looking good is vital. Tones of peach and apricot suit you well, and you wear them with flair and panache. Diamonds are a Rooster's best friend and, for you, the bigger, the better.

You shine at social gatherings. Witty, entertaining and full of tall tales, you love being the life of the party. There is always a crowd around you, and you love it.

However, you are just as comfortable around your coop, which you've organized with love and care. Everything has a place and neatness is important. Cleaning is your passion and you have the habit of constantly rearranging the furniture – which may drive your family crazy.

In the outside world, your temperament is suited for a career as an administrative assistant or a financial advisor. You may also want to join a theater group to refine your dramatic flair. If you can sing or dance, you should consider pursuing your talents in these fields.

Once you have a brood to cluck over, you make a great Hen. Your natural instinct is to protect the little ones, but sometimes you are too zealous in this department. Since you cannot tolerate bad manners, your punishments are harsh. You use old-fashioned standards for discipline, which may be too severe at times.

IF YOU LOVE A MALE ROOSTER

He's as proud as a peacock, strutting around in his flashy clothes and jewelry. He is opinionated and macho – a regular show-off – impressing others with his style and charm.

He is downright honest, which could hurt your feelings at times. He says what's on his mind and doesn't mince his words – he's not known for being diplomatic. The good news is that he is not a trickster, like the Monkey.

At times, the male Rooster may appear blunt, bossy and rude. This may be due to the mood swings to which he is prone. Since Roosters are go-getters, always on the move and always in the limelight, their stress levels run high. The exacting standards they set for themselves makes things worse. So when they let loose, it's not a pretty sight.

While male Roosters are great advice-givers when it comes to money matters, they don't do as well with their own finances. They often have a hard time sticking to a budget. Instead, they like to blow their bank account on "boy toys" – a car or a big-screen television.

On the home front, he will rule the roost with an iron fist. Although he loves his children deeply, he is stern and intolerant when his offspring get rambunctious. He will not tolerate a fresh mouth.

In the love department, he is a strong and forceful lover. Although he may strut around attracting attention, once he finds what he wants, he will settle down to a faithful relationship – but don't think it means he won't be looking at other women. He cannot help himself.

IF YOU ARE A MALE ROOSTER

Proud and elegant, you are confident and cheerful. You have the amazing ability to bounce back when life gets you down. Your wit and innate good humor carries you through the bad times and shows your courage.

Protecting your ladylove is of the utmost importance. It goes with your macho image. You think nothing of going head-to-head with somebody who is pestering or hurting her.

Patience is not a virtue with you. You have a short fuse, but your outbursts flare quickly and your feathers are soon smoothed.

Driven by ambition, you stick to your goals and don't rest until they have been attained. Your dogged determination is admired by co-workers and supervisors alike. That drive makes you a natural for a career in the military, the police, marketing or selling insurance. However, your natural flamboyance makes you an ideal candidate for politics or acting.

You tend to see the world in black and white – right and wrong. There is little middle ground for compromise. Your beliefs are conservative, and you have little tolerance for those who think otherwise.

Despite this attitude, you have a warm heart and you want to be loved by others – even if you don't show it. It will take a special lady to break through the barriers you have erected around you. Once she does, you are capable of giving and receiving a deep and abiding love.

IF YOU LOVE A FEMALE ROOSTER

Female Roosters are feisty and honest. She has an outgoing personality and an entourage of acquaintances. In her trendy clothes and stylish hair, she cuts a striking figure and is a knockout in any crowd.

Drama comes easily to the female Rooster. She can play up any problem to the max, hoping that her shining knight will bail her out. But if he doesn't, she'll take care of things herself.

She has the courage to stand behind her convictions. Don't expect her to back down easily. She speaks out passionately for her current cause and lets everyone know how she feels.

The female Rooster loves her home. It is decorated in a traditional decor, with no clutter and a place for everything. She dotes on keeping it clean and neat. You will find it a pleasure coming home, except that the furniture may not be where you last saw it. Redecorating is a pastime the Hen enjoys enormously.

The Hen's temperament is to spend, spend, spend. Only the best will do, and her tastes are expensive. She can spend hours at the mall, or better yet, at trendy shops.

It's also in her character to want to be the boss. This tendency to take over may rub you the wrong way, but it is mellowed by her willingness to bend over backwards to help others.

While she may seem highly critical of others, including you, she wants to be loved and she is anxious to please.

AWESOME UNIONS

Rooster & Ox: Mutual respect and admiration make this a winning combination. They motivate and support each other. The Ox is attracted by the Rooster's style, and the Rooster honors the Ox's determination. Conflict may occur when the Rooster goes on a spending spree, but if the Ox's practical advice is taken into consideration, these two can have a happy, long-lasting union.

Rooster & Snake: Intellectually, these two signs are well matched. The Rooster is more domineering, but the Snake's calm demeanor is a good antidote. The Rooster likes being seduced by the Snake's charm, and the Snake enjoys the Rooster's posturing. When the Rooster's temper gets going, the Snake knows how to disappear until the storm has blown over.

Rooster & Horse: Power conflicts are the one element that can destroy this pair. While there is often a physical attraction, in the long run, the road can get rocky as the squabbling begins. It's best for these two to go their separate ways business-wise. In a marriage, there will have to be a good deal of give and take, with a clear division of responsibilities and lots of support.

Great:
Ox, Snake, Horse
Neutral:
Goat, Pig, Tiger, Dragon
Challenging:
Rat, Rabbit, Monkey, Rooster, Dog

THE DOG

YEARS
1922
1934
1946
1958
1970
1982
1994

Like man's best friend, loyalty is the key element of the Dog's personality. They are dependable, no-nonsense people who are sincere and good-natured. They hate hypocrisy and pretentiousness.

Down-to-earth and honest as they come, Dogs are governed by a keen sense of right and wrong. They can quickly assess a person's character, and they don't bother with those people they don't care for. These strong-willed individuals stand up for the causes they believe in.

The Dog may not be as ambitious as the Dragon or the Rooster, and the Dog may not have the clever mind of the Monkey. But when it comes to a loving and devoted partner, a Dog is steadfast and selfless and aims to please.

It is rare that Dogs rush into marriage. Instead, they want a relationship to develop over time and blossom into a fruitful union.

IF YOU ARE A FEMALE DOG

This Lassie is a giver, not a taker. You always have a kind word to say to others. One of your greatest assets is you find time to listen to everyone's problems, even when you have your own things to do. But you rarely discuss your troubles with anyone else. Instead, you bottle things up inside and worry in private.

Friends and strangers often find it discomforting when you walk into a new situation and try to take over. It's simply in your character to give advice when none has been asked for. But don't fret. Your generosity, good nature and genuine concern comes through to dispel any ill feelings.

Being happy is your best defense against getting sick. Walking in the park or on the beach gives you the low-impact exercise you prefer. High-energy games such as tennis, racquetball and soccer are not for you. Neither is a marathon run. Instead, you like to take it slow and easy with swimming, yoga and the step machines.

While female Dogs make wonderful mothers, they don't just want to stay at home. Giving is second nature and you will find fulfillment as a nurse or doctor, teacher, caregiver, clergywoman or magistrate. Like your male counterpart, you are a good judge of character, which will help you in any of these professions.

Anybody that has you for a friend should consider him or herself lucky. You are solid, sensible and reliable. In a crisis, you make yourself available, no matter what else is pressing on your time and energy. Your priorities are always in order.

Your only fault is that when you find flaws in others, you may be less than tactful. Telling the truth can hurt feelings, and you should be careful when giving honest advice or criticism.

On the plus side, you are a devoted mother to your little pups. You will do anything to protect them from harm, and you give selflessly when they are ill or in need of your attention. When your pups are involved with sports activities, you are there rooting for them all the way.

IF YOU LOVE A MALE DOG

He thinks he knows best. And sometimes he does, but other times he doesn't have a clue. However, he's a hard worker and a good provider. Although it may have taken him some time to decide on a career path, once he is on the scent, he'll work diligently toward his ultimate goal.

You're in luck if you've chosen to spend your life with a male Dog. He is wise with his money, investing it for the future and not squandering it on wasteful things. Unlike the Rooster who needs his toys, the male Dog knows how to live comfortably and conserve at the same time. Your later years will be financially secure and the best part is that you won't have to scrimp.

Vacations won't cost a fortune, either. The male Dog is content to sit and watch the world go by. He doesn't need thrills or spills to have a good time. And he isn't looking to go off to the woods by himself. He's an easygoing guy when it comes to kicking back and relaxing on the beach or at a country resort. Being a family man, he enjoys having his kids around for a visit to a theme park or just to do nothing but throw a Frisbee™ and hit a few balls.

Don't expect any fireworks from the male Dog, though. He takes life as it comes and he goes with the flow. Status and wealth are not as important as being happy. Fortunately for you, he wants his loved ones to be as content as he is. He'll bend over backward to fill your needs.

You may find him on the shy side. That's because he's getting to know you better without rushing into things. Progressing at a slow and steady pace, this relationship will blossom over time. He also doesn't want to get hurt and it's in his character to be a little anxious. So don't expect any rash proposals. He won't sweep you off your feet like a Dragon might, but once he makes up his mind, he'll be devoted and steadfast.

IF YOU ARE A MALE DOG

*Y*ou tend to be somewhat of a worrier. However, you are reliable and resourceful. As you make your way steadily up the corporate ladder, you are not unwilling to lending a helping hand to those who deserve it. This willingness to share your good fortune and assist others makes you a popular guy. You play for the team, which people admire.

Occupations that suit you best are civil service and teaching positions. Since you are a good judge of character, you are a qualified candidate for becoming a teacher, clergyman or social service worker. Your compassion for others will bring you success in any of these fields.

Socializing is a large part of your life, but you prefer small dinner parties to full-blown galas. You enjoy carrying on a conversation instead of shouting over loud music. When you find yourself at a lavish function, you will withdraw and sit alone or with one other person, instead of mingling. In any case, you are an attentive listener.

Playing the field isn't your thing. You know what's important – coming home to a comfortable house at the end of a long day, with dinner waiting and a lively companion who'll lend a sympathetic ear. So once you've found your soulmate, there is no more fooling around. Home is where the heart is.

As far as your pups are concerned, you're there for them all the way. Whether it's taking them to practice, cheering them on during matches, or wiping their tears if they lose, you are a dad 100 percent. You will instill in them self-reliance, loyalty and compassion. No matter how old they are, or how far away they move, they'll know you will come through for them.

IF YOU LOVE A FEMALE DOG

She's a worrier. She frets over small things and often appears anxious and distracted. However, she is faithful and honest. She values your love and friendship and will, in turn, repay any kindness.

Her home will be filled with love. Neat and orderly, the female Dog takes pride in her den. While there is nothing showy or ostentatious, the Dog's home is comfortable, decorated with wood, wool and traditional pieces instead of high-tech or modern furniture. You may look for dust in the Dog's house, but you won't find any. She spends hours vacuuming and polishing.

The female Dog knows how to dress neatly and conservatively. She doesn't go overboard when it comes to spending money on clothes, yet she always is well-groomed. This is not a high-maintenance woman. If you plan to buy jewelry, forget the diamonds and get her a carnelian or something made with amber or topaz.

Female Dogs are wonderful mothers. You couldn't ask for a better mom for your pups. She gives her offspring a sense of fair play and compassion that will serve them well in later life.

In a marriage, she is a true companion, helpful and supportive, tender and loving. Her needs are small and her heart is big. Female Dogs are anxious to please and they are adept at making a cozy home. What more could anyone ask?

AWESOME UNIONS

Dog & Tiger: The Dog admires the Tiger's courage. The Tiger benefits from the Dog's dependable nature. Both share many interests, which makes this a stable union and a steady business partnership. The Tiger will dispel the Dog's worry and will profit from the Dog's wise counsel when it comes to taking risks. Although there are personality differences, both are loyal and trusting. Together, they provide a harmonious environment to raise their pups.

Dog & Horse: These hard-workers can find happiness together as a married couple or as business partners. Each is mindful of the other's viewpoint. While the Dog tends to be cautious and the Horse rash, they are enterprising and resourceful. Physical attraction will be the initial turn-on. Later, they will find that common interests strengthen the bonds between them.

Dog & Monkey: At first glance, this may appear to be a mismatched union. The Monkey is quick and agile. The Dog is slower and a worrier. However, as they get to know each other better, they will find that they can benefit from their differences. The lively Monkey alleviates the Dog's worry. The Dog's loyalty and affection make the Monkey secure in the marriage. With open communication and support, disputes can be worked out.

Dog & Dog: The only drawback to this winning combination is worry, with both partners anxious and fretting. Other than that, this is an almost-perfect union. Both value the same things in life. Neither is a spendthrift, and both know the importance of family. When hard times roll around, Dogs know that if they can weather the storm, they will thrive as long as they stick together.

LOVE MATCHES

Great:
Tiger, Horse, Monkey, Dog

Neutral:
Pig, Rabbit, Snake, Rat, Ox

Challenging:
Dragon, Goat, Rooster

THE PIG

YEARS
1923
1935
1947
1959
1971
1983
1995

In the West, calling someone a pig is not considered polite. But in the Orient, the pig is sincere, honest, genial and hard-working – all positive attributes.

Pigs love people and look for charitable causes and help those less fortunate with their good deeds. However, this trusting nature is often abused by those who want to take advantage.

Pigs are known for being peacemakers and avoiding confrontations at all costs. They are not vindictive, nor do they harbor grudges.

In money matters, they have the capacity to earn a lot, but they also like spending it. And they take great delight in buying presents for others. Having company over for dinner is a cause for celebration. They like nothing better than to break out the best for their close friends.

When it comes to love, the Pig is passionate and sensual – a pleasure seeker who throws him or herself into marriage with abandon.

IF YOU ARE A FEMALE PIG

You were born with a cheerful, outgoing and patient personality. Your greatest delight is brightening up other peoples' lives. By nature, you are kind and caring.

Harmony plays an important part in your life. Conflicts cause you stress. While some signs thrive on chaos, you prefer peace and quiet.

The occupations that suit you best are teaching, designing, window dressing, floral arranging and nutritionist – but you are not as career-minded as some of the other signs. Each of these professions will draw on your attention to detail, an area in which you excel. But none of these require much physical exertion, so you'll have to make time for that on your own in order to maintain a healthy balance.

Pigs are domestic creatures so piglets will get your undivided attention. You'll spoil your little ones, but you will insist on good manners. While you are at home, you enjoy gardening, craftwork and reading. In truth, you like being home better than at work.

If you don't have a full-time job, you will be called upon to participate in the PTA and various civic groups. Be careful not to overcommit or you'll find yourself stressed, which goes against your placid nature. Leave plenty of time for your family and yourself.

You make a wonderful partner to snuggle up to. You give your affection generously and ask little in return. When you find the right partner, your passion will turn the burners on high.

IF YOU LOVE A MALE PIG

The male Pig is generous, diligent and sincere. On the other hand, he may be pigheaded at times. This stubborn streak, combined with his tendency for laziness, are his only unflattering attributes.

It's easy to take advantage of a Pig's good nature. He is dependable, and you may begin to take him for granted. This would be a mistake. For while a male Pig loves to give, he does not want to be trampled upon, and when he draws the line, you'll know it.

Don't expect the male Pig to settle for the cheapest model automobile or boat. He is an extravagant creature who likes the very best. Shelling out large sums won't put him in the poorhouse, but the male Pig would do well thinking about the future – and not only the moment. If he could learn to tone down his taste, then his retirement years wouldn't be such a stretch financially.

Since he loves company and delights in having people over, the male Pig makes the perfect host. He is engaging and witty, serving the best wines and unusual gourmet meals. Before company arrives, he will be in the kitchen cooking up a storm, experimenting with gastronomic delights.

Male pigs make excellent fathers. While they won't be out at the park playing sports, they will frequent museums and the movies, spending loads of time together with the piglets.

In their younger years, male Pigs are known for playing the field. They have a healthy interest in sexual matters. However, once they settle down, they make caring and loyal partners.

IF YOU'RE A MALE PIG

At work you are suited to a wide range of occupations, including the fields of health, communications, design, teaching and the restaurant business. Every job that you tackle is done with method and precision. Chipping away at monumental projects delights you. When they are completed, you have something solid to show for your effort.

When it comes to your health, you tend to be sedentary and self-indulgent. Exercise is not high on your list of priorities, which means that health problems will plague you.

Vacations must include sumptuous food and exotic drinks. France would be the ideal choice for a Pig's getaway, but a cruise will do. Holidays are the best time for self-indulgence, and since you work hard, you deserve it.

You expect others to be as honest and straightforward as you are. When they're not, you are sorely disappointed. Your biggest character flaws are that you are gullible and you tend to take the easy way out. You are certainly not a go-getter, working overtime. But as long as you earn a decent living, you feel life is to be cherished.

It may take a while for you to enter into a committed relationship. Settling down at an early age may leave too many stones unturned. But once you do, you'll likely invest in a hot tub so you can enjoy the sensuality of a relaxing soaking with your lady.

IF YOU LOVE A FEMALE PIG

She likes her creature comforts. Be prepared to pamper the female Pig. She's a material girl who wants to impress others. After she has worked long and hard to decorate her home in style, she may sit back on the couch and forget about keeping it tidy. This is the female Pig's dual nature. It doesn't do any good to question it. Acceptance is the only road to peace and harmony.

If you like eating, you will delight in the female Pig's creativity in the kitchen. Cooking is her joy and she loves watching others savor her culinary abilities. She is a charming hostess, making sure everybody has had enough to eat and sending home leftovers with the guests. And don't worry if your friends drop in unexpectedly. She is a whiz at whipping up something to eat in a pinch.

Female Pigs are not known for their interest in exercise. While their health is generally robust, they are prone to digestive problems and weight gain. Since they like the company of others, joining a gym would be a great way to maintain good health while socializing.

Don't believe for a minute that because she isn't an exercise nut, that Pigs aren't actively passionate or sensual. Pigs are sensual by nature, and female Pigs expect their lovemaking to be passionate and intense. She is a bundle of love if you can keep up with her.

AWESOME UNIONS

Pig & Rabbit: These two sociable signs get along well together. Pigs are lucky in business, and the Rabbit is shrewd, which makes them a fortunate duo. Both enjoy the beauty of nature, and both are peace-loving creatures. There is a strong physical attraction between these two signs, which can lead to a harmonious and stable marriage.

Pig & Goat: The robust Pig feels comfortable with the Goat's easygoing disposition. The Goat likes the Pig's domestic side. These two relaxed signs both have sensual natures, which means their romantic passions are kept on high most of the time. They work well as a team, both in business ventures and in raising a family.

Pig & Rat: While this may look like the odd couple at first glance, the Pig and Rat make a formidable pair. The Pig's ability to move steadily toward a goal, and the Rat's skill in seeking out new opportunities, makes for a money-making team. Both the Rat and the Pig have outgoing personalities that mesh well together. With a mutual attraction, these two good-looking signs can make a comfy, cozy home.

LOVE MATCHES

Great:
Rabbit, Goat, Rat
Just Average:
Ox, Horse, Dog, Dragon, Rooster
Challenging:
Snake, Pig, Monkey, Tiger

WESTERN COUNTERPARTS

Now that you know what each of the Chinese Love Signs mean, see how they compare to the familiar Western astrological signs.

Which one describes you the best?

The Rat = Sagittarius
The Ox = Capricorn
The Tiger = Aquarius
The Rabbit = Pisces
The Dragon = Aries
The Snake = Taurus
The Horse = Gemini
The Goat = Cancer
The Monkey = Leo
The Rooster = Virgo
The Dog = Libra
The Pig = Scorpio

MISMATCHED SIGNS

The Rat & The Tiger

Clashes will occur over money matters. The Tiger is generous and the Rat is thrifty. In addition, the Tiger's restless nature will make the Rat feel unsettled. Although they may have mutual interests, a union would be filled with tension and problems.

The Rat & The Goat

While there may be a mutual attraction, obstacles will soon arise. The Rat is hardworking and industrious, while the Goat is more leisurely. The Rat is thrifty, the Goat can be a spender. The Rat's honesty may hurt the Goat's feelings, and the Rat may lose patience with the Goat's whimsical, artistic nature. In turn, the Goat will see the Rat as meddlesome and fussy. It may take too great an effort to make this match work.

The Ox & The Tiger

This union will be difficult to maintain – even with give and take on both sides. While the Ox may be initially attracted to the Tiger's wild side, the Ox's conservative outlook would be constantly challenged. The Tiger likes action and lots of it. The Ox prefers calm activities and an orderly life. Whereas the Tiger is sociable, the Ox is not. They move at different speeds and in different ways. Money is another sore spot. The Tiger likes to spend while the Ox is prudent. Since both are stubborn and strong-willed, there is little likelihood this union will work.

The Ox & The Horse

These two signs do not relate well to each other. They have few common interests. Each wants to dominate the relationship, and neither will compromise. The Horse is active, while the Ox is passive. The Horse likes to roam, and the Ox prefers to stay at home. The Horse cherishes independence, which the Ox does not understand. When tempers flare, and they often will, there is no concession on either side. And when it comes to making up, the Horse will find that the Ox lacks passion.

The Tiger & The Snake

The Tiger is an extrovert, filled with energy and passion. The Snake is an introvert, calm, orderly and reflective. They have little in common, and the Snake will quickly tire of the Tiger's hustle and bustle. Likewise, the Tiger will resent the Snake's possessiveness. There will be little trust between these two and, with rare exceptions, the relationship will not last.

The Monkey & The Tiger

At first passion runs high between these two signs. But while the Tiger is honest and forthright, the Monkey is evasive and crafty. The Monkey likes to keep tabs on everything, and the Tiger resents the interference. Since both are competitive, a power struggle will certainly occur. Their domineering personalities and spirited nature will make this pair a poor bet for the long haul.

The Rat & The Rabbit

While there may be a strong physical attraction, in terms of a marriage, these signs are ill-suited for one another. The Rat is active and energetic. The Rabbit is quiet and settled. When the Rat is honest, it may hurt the sensitive Rabbit's feelings. The Rat may find the Rabbit's cautious nature restricting, and the Rabbit will certainly find the Rat's behavior brash and irritating. It would take a major effort for the Rat to become more refined and the Rabbit to be more outgoing. Both parties would have to make major adjustments for the marriage to work.

The Rooster & The Rabbit

There is nothing in common between these two. The Rooster is too candid for the shy Rabbit. Even as business partners, this is not a good match. In a romance, the Rooster will be too rash and wild for the Rabbit. The Rabbit likes peace and quiet while the Rooster is constantly on the go, with bluster and bravado. In every aspect, from dress to home decor, this couple is a complete mismatch.

The Dragon & The Dog

The Dog sees the Dragon as opinionated, while the Dragon has little patience for the serious hound. The Dragon is the domineering one, and the Dog is critical of the Dragon's risk-taking. They often pull in opposite directions, both in business and in bed. The Dragon's showiness does not impress the Dog. And to the Dragon, the Dog seems like a drab mate. The Dragon gives the Dog plenty to worry about and little solace. Both are stubborn. In money matters, the Dog is practical, saving for a rainy day. The Dragon is just the opposite. There is little compromise and even less chance for a smooth ride in an alliance.

The Pig & The Snake

The good-natured, honest Pig will find it difficult to relate to the Snake's evasive nature. While the Pig delights in entertaining dinner guests, the Snake feels ill at ease and will slither away, leaving the Pig holding the bag. While this is not an impossible situation, it will take much work on both parts to have the Snake join the Pig at a party. And the Pig must keep an open mind when it comes to the Snake's preference for a solitary existence.

The Rooster & The Goat

This pair is not well-suited at all. The Rooster is efficient and practical. The Goat is carefree and easygoing. As business partners, trouble will soon arise. The Rooster is a planner, an organizer and a hard-worker. The Goat is laid-back and lacks discipline. In a marriage, the sensitive Goat may find the Rooster too fussy and critical. The Rooster finds the Goat's whimsical nature too pretentious and silly. Since both like to spend money, they can plow through their savings in no time, leaving nothing for tomorrow – if there is a tomorrow.

1998 ASTROLOGICAL CALENDARS
WITH *PERSONALIZED* DAILY FORECASTS

- ★ **Original Paintings by the world renowned artist George di Carlo**
- ★ **Choose from ALL signs of the Zodiac**
- ★ **Your best Love Matches, Lucky Numbers & MORE**

ONLY $9.95 U.S.

A great gift! SAVE! SAVE! SAVE!
Order 2 or more for only $8.95 each.

ORDER TODAY!

Mail to: Globe Calendar Offer, P.O. Box 114, Rouses Point, NY 12979-0114

Yes! Send the Calendar(s) I've indicated below. I've enclosed $9.95 ($10.95 Canadian) plus $.99 each for postage & handling. SAVE! SAVE! SAVE! Order 2 or more & enclose $8.95 for each ($9.95 Canadian) plus $.99 each for postage & handling.

My check, payable to Globe Calendar, is enclosed for $_____

Name_____

Address_____

City_____

State_____ Zip_____

Indicate number desired of each calendar →

___Aries   ___Cancer   ___Libra   ___Capricorn
___Taurus ___Leo   ___Scorpio   ___Aquarius
___Gemini ___Virgo   ___Sagittarius ___Pisces

*Please allow 4 to 8 weeks for delivery.
FL and NY residents, please add sales tax.*

GD43